IMAGES
of England

Sheffield United Football Club

IMAGES
of England

SHEFFIELD UNITED FOOTBALL CLUB

Compiled by
Denis Clarebrough

First published 1998

Tempus Publishing Limited
The Mill, Brimscombe Port,
Stroud, Gloucestershire, GL5 2QG

ISBN 0 7524 1059 8

Typesetting and origination by
Tempus Publishing Limited
Printed in Great Britain by
Bailey Print, Dursley, Gloucestershire

Present and forthcoming titles by Tempus Publishing:

Bristol Rovers FC
Bury FC
Cardiff City FC 1899-1947
Cardiff City FC 1947-1971
Charlton Athletic FC
Exeter City FC
Newport County AFC
Oxford United FC
Plymouth Argyle FC
Reading FC
Sunderland FC

Contents

Acknowledgements

I would like to thank Sheffield Newspapers, for granting permission to use photographs and cartoons, and those former Sheffield United directors, staff, players and supporters who have been so generous in loaning photographs and memorabilia. I will also take this opportunity to pay tribute to the many club historians and collectors – the majority of whom are members of The Association of Football Statisticians and Football Postcard Collectors Club – for their kind assistance.

Bramall Lane before 1895. This photograph shows the old cycle track which was removed in 1901.

Introduction

I was delighted to be asked to put together this collection of Sheffield United photographs and illustrations of assorted memorabilia. I began my collection as a boy, with newspaper cuttings and war-time programmes. I inherited from my father a passion for, and devotion to, Sheffield United. However, as he so often told me in an attempt, as a good Yorkshireman, to pass on to me the virtues of thrift, he had never bought a programme in his life, so any United memorabilia would have to be collated through my own efforts. No doubt his heart sank when, in early ventures to the Lane, I discovered that the club issued a match programme.

Despite this early enthusiasm, the bulk of my collection has been put together in the last sixteen years or so, as I looked for items that could be used to illustrate articles in the United programme and the centenary history of the club.

The club's badge, which appeared on shirts in the 1891/92 season.

Roll Of Honour

Football League Champions
Division One 1897-98
Division Two 1952-53
Division Four 1981-82

F A Cup Winners
1899
1902
1915
1925

One

The Early Years: 1889-1896

Adding football to cricket

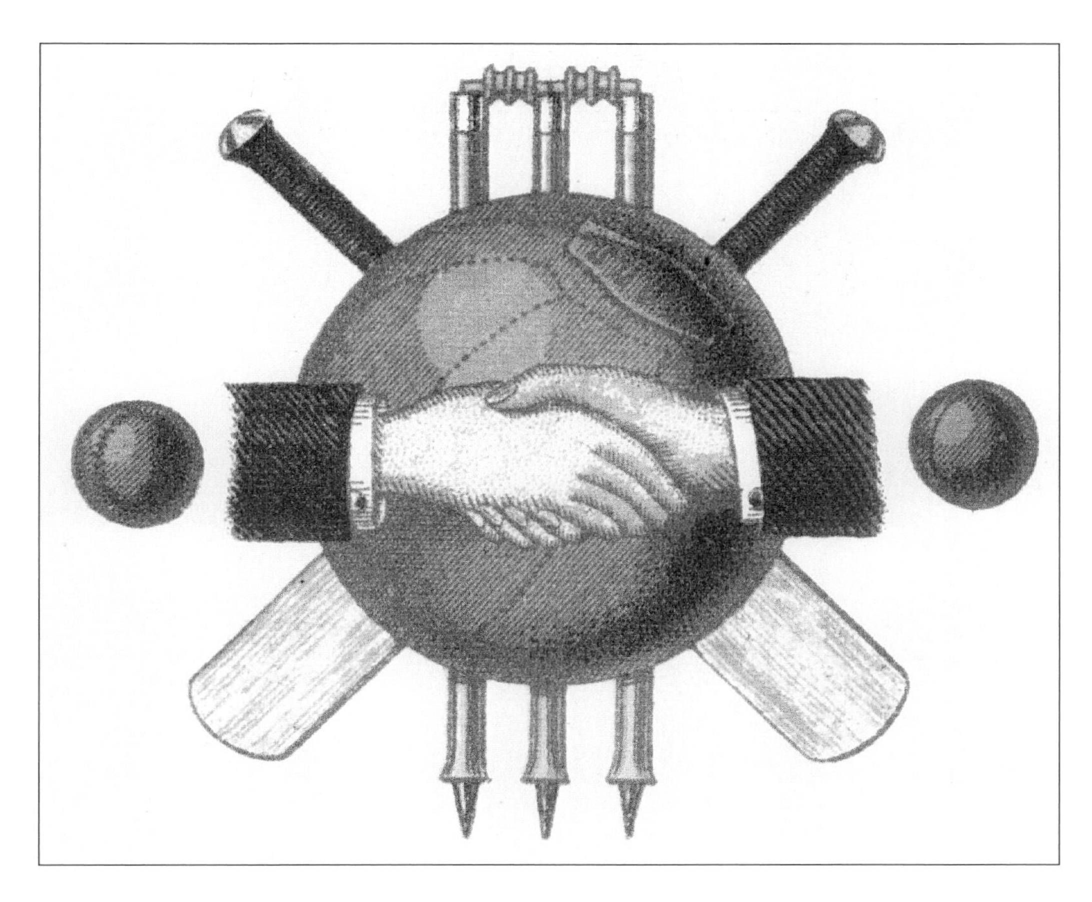

The ground at Bramall Lane had been built in 1855 for cricket and the first football match was played there in 1862. It was increasingly used for important football matches during the 1880s, including those of the Wednesday Football Club. The developing popularity of association football and the decision of the Wednesday to build their own ground at Olive Grove, led the committee who ran the ground at Bramall Lane to form a football club, which would be called Sheffield United.

The football side of the ground, 1889. The tower of St Mary's church can be clearly seen behind the main stand. The track around the playing area was used for athletics and cycling.

For their first season, United fielded a team of local and Scottish professionals, assisted by amateurs from the Sheffield Football Club. The best-known player was the outside left, Billy Mosforth, who had played for the Wednesday and had nine England caps.

The earliest known photograph of Sheffield United Football Club. United had worn white shirts in their first season but added a narrow red stripe for the 1890/91 campaign, when this photograph was taken. Three players are wearing the badge, and one the cap, of the Sheffield and Hallamshire Football Association. The club had their first taste of league football in the Midland Counties League. The stern-faced gentleman on the back row was J. B. Wostinholm, Secretary of the Yorkshire County Cricket Club, which was administered from Sheffield in those days, as well as the United Football and Cricket Club.

A sketch of the ground, 1891. Note the temporary stand on the cricket side, erected for the FA Cup semi-final between Notts County and Sunderland.

United entered the Northern League in 1891/92 and, from this side, the foundations of the team that would play such a leading role at the turn of the century were laid. A major influence was the signing and appointment as club captain of Billy Hendry (middle row, looking away from the camera). His advice and example was to play a large part in the development of Ernest Needham, who would turn out to be one of United's greatest players.

OFFICERS.

PRESIDENT.
M. J. ELLISON, ESQ.

VICE-PRESIDENT.
M. ELLISON, JUN., ESQ.

COMMITTEE.
The GROUND COMMITTEE, and
Messrs. J. SMITH, W. F. BEARDSHAW, J. TOMLINSON,
G. J. GROVES, T. B. A. CLARKE, J. BEARDSHAW.

HON. MEDICAL OFFICER.
J. STOKES, M.D.,
82, Ecclesall Road, Sheffield.

PARTICULARS.

Committee meet in the Bramall Lane Pavilion, on the Ground, each Tuesday night, at Six o'clock.

CLUB HOUSE:—MAUNCHE HOTEL,
E. TWIVEY, PROPRIETOR.

COLOURS OF THE CLUB.
BLUE KNICKERS, WHITE SHIRT WITH RED STRIPE.

BYE-LAWS.

1.—Every player, whether amateur or professional, shall appear in proper football costume, both when practising and engaged in a match on behalf of the Club, and no member will be permitted to practice or play on the ground unless wearing the authorised costume of the Club.

2.—No practice will be permitted under any circumstances on days when matches are played, either before or after the match.

3.—All reasonable commands of the Captain in the field must be promptly obeyed. He shall have power to alter the positions of the players if during the progress of the match he thinks it advisable to do so.

4.—The team shall be complete before leaving the dressing room, and must come on the field in a body led by the Captain at least 5 minutes before advertised time of kick off, unless otherwise instructed by the Secretary.

5.—All articles for the use of the members, provided by the Committee, are the property of the Club.

6.—The Captain shall return the ball to the Storekeeper immediately on the conclusion of the match.

An extract from the booklet issued to the players for the 1891/92 season.

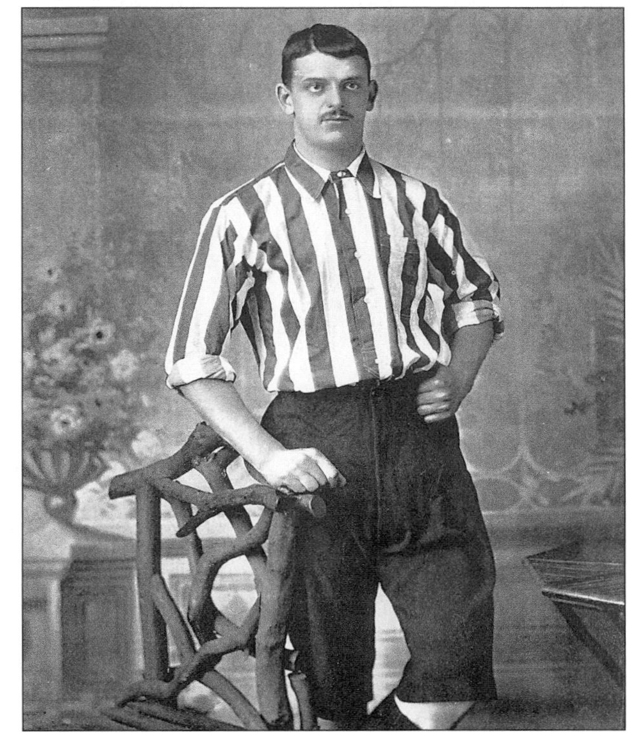

Elected to the Football League in 1892, United were promoted to the First Division at the end of that first season, after a test match victory over Accrington in Nottingham. Mick Whitham, a stalwart of the defence and an ever-present in the League that season was the first of several United internationals who had played for Ecclesfield, a village team, five miles north of Sheffield.

Terrier-like in his tackling and blessed with tremendous stamina, Rab Howell, another former Ecclesfield player, who along with Hendry and Needham (and later with Morren) formed a diminutive, but highly effective, half-back line.

These 1894/95 players included a new goalkeeper, Bill Foulke, who would become one of the great celebrities of English football.

Arthur Wharton, the reserve-team goalkeeper, has the distinction of being the first coloured professional footballer. He had previously appeared in the colours of Preston North End and Rotherham Town.

SHEFFIELD UNITED FOOTBALL CLUB.

NEW YEAR'S TOUR.

		GOALS FOR	GOALS AGST.
Dec. 29.	At Bolton: v. Bolton Wanderers		
Dec. 31.	At Glasgow: v. Clyde		
Jan. 1.	At Leith: v. Leith Athletic ...		
Jan. 2.	At Dundee: v. Dundee		
Jan. 3.	At Kirkcaldy: v. Raith Rovers ...		

Saturday, December 29th.

Train leaves Victoria Station for Bolton at 8-50 in the morning, arriving at Manchester at 10 o'clock.

Lunch at "Sam's Chop House" at 11-15.

Leave Manchester for Bolton at 12 o'clock, arriving at Bolton at 12-20.

Match commences at 2 o'clock.

After match leave Bolton, L. & Y. Rly. at 5-50. Dine in the Dining Car. Arrive at Glasgow "Central" at 10-45 p.m.

Proceed to the Old Waverley Temperance Hotel, Buchanan Street, for night.

A feature of the 1894/95 season was what United called the 'Scotch' Tour. A sad outcome of these matches was an injury to Billy Hendry that brought his days with the club to an end.

Ernest Needham, the 'Prince of Half Backs' took over the mantle of captain. A superb all-round player and automatic choice for England

Bill Foulke, the giant United goalkeeper. In spite of his ever-increasing weight, which rose to over twenty stones, Foulke remained an excellent keeper. Always a showman, crowds flocked to marvel at the distance he could kick and fist the ball.

Two

The Golden Years: 1897-1904

The League and two cups

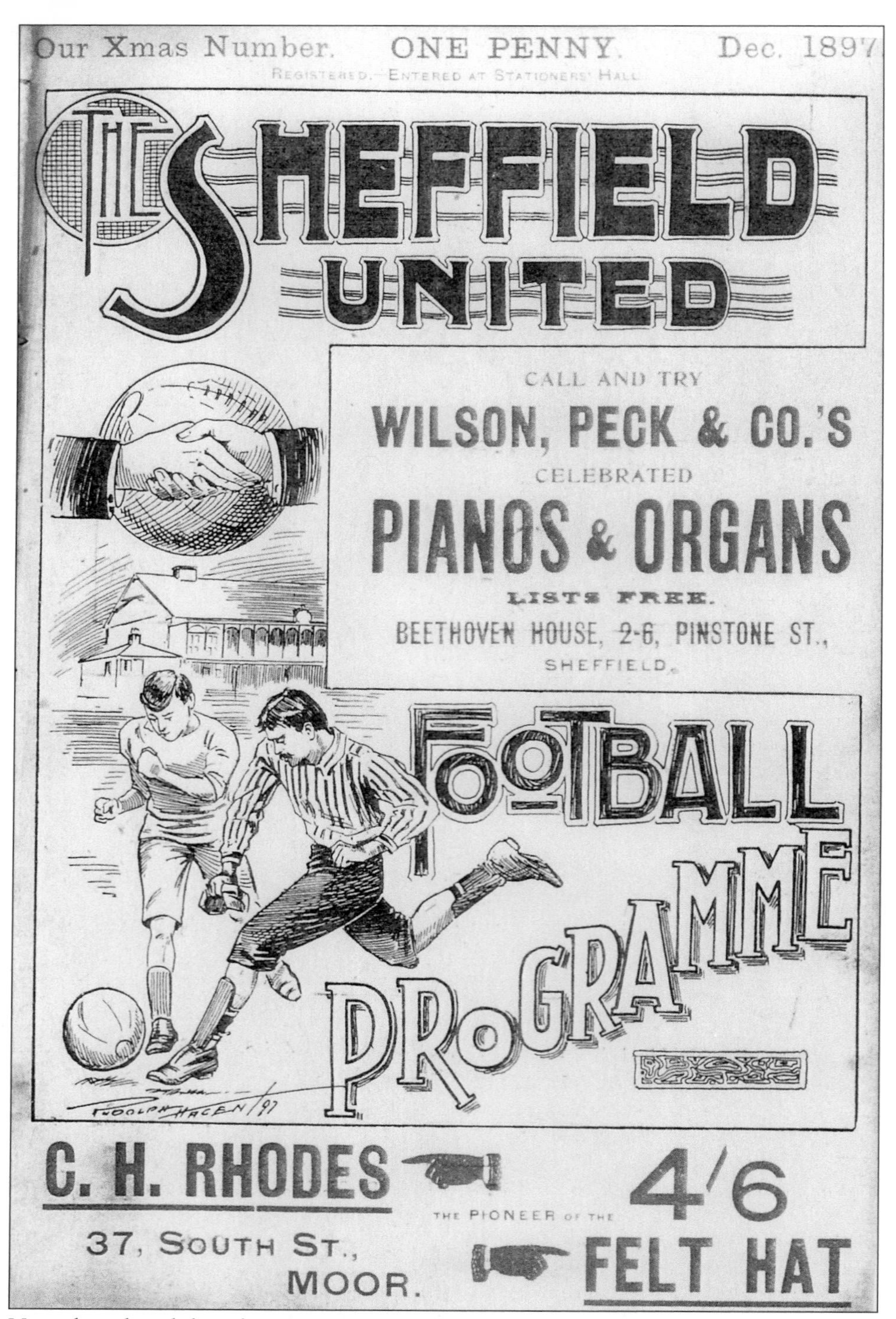

United produced their first programmes for the 1897/98 season. The first few were of only eight pages, but it was soon doubled in size. Prior to this, occasional match cards had been produced and sold by Billy Whitham, who also sold cricket scorecards for matches at the Lane.

United's only First Division championship success came in 1898, after finishing second in the previous season. Ten of the players who took part in the success were present, or future, English internationals.

Tommy Morren, a centre half of only five feet and five inches in height, joined United in November 1895 from Middlesbrough, where he had won an amateur cup medal. He had been asked to sign as a professional for Reading, but United were tipped off as to the move and persuaded Morren to leave his train when it stopped at Sheffield. He then signed for United. He completed an all-international half-back line of Howell, Morren and Needham (all of whom were less than five feet six inches in height).

Players, committee members and officials with the First Division Championship trophy and the Sheriff of London Charity Shield. United were also the unofficial champions of Great Britain, having defeated Glasgow Celtic in challenge matches.

United began the 1898/99 season as champions of the First Division and would end it as FA cup winners. The John Street stand, that comprises the background of the picture, had been built in 1895 and had 2,000 seats – but this soon proved inadequate.

A First Division Championship flag flies aloft over the Shoreham Street stand, which had been built in 1897. Severely damaged by a gale in 1903, it was subsequently demolished.

United's 4-1 Cup Final victory over Derby County in 1899, as seen by *The London Illustrated News*.

The United players return to Sheffield after their first Cup Final success. Needham holds the cup at the front and Foulke sits above the nearest rear wheel.

The successful Cup team of 1899, from left to right, back row: Hedley, Beer, Thickett, Foulke, Almond and Boyle. Front row: Bennett, Johnson, Needham, Morren and Priest.

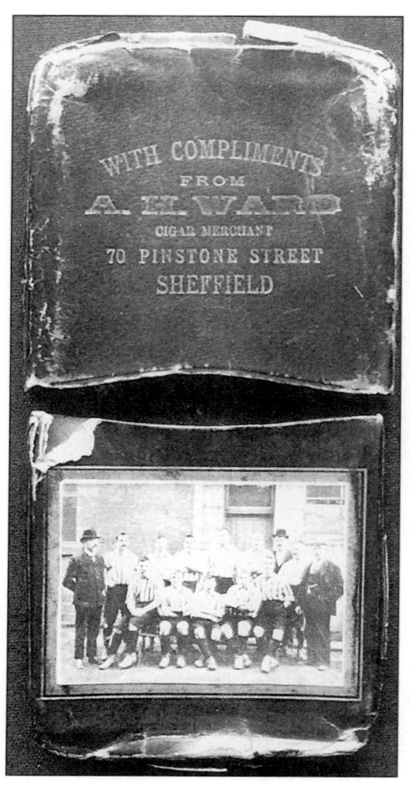

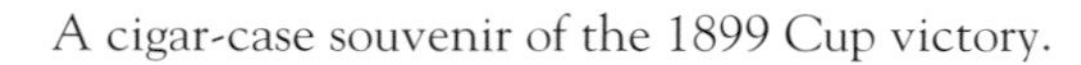

A cigar-case souvenir of the 1899 Cup victory.

The United team included four players who came from the North East of England. Fred Priest, a great-hearted player, came from South Bank. Priest first played for United in 1896, mainly at outside left but later at inside forward, in which role he formed a fine left-wing partnership with Bert Lipsham. Determined and tenacious, he was a player for the big occasion, often scoring invaluable goals in cup ties.

George Hedley, the centre forward, was another former South Bank player. He added a third FA Cup winner's medal to the two he won with United, when playing for Wolverhampton Wanderers in 1908.

Peter Boyle, the left back and Irish international, was transferred to United from Sunderland in 1898. His son, Tommy, would play for United in the 1925 Cup Final. Cigarette cards such as this were a popular new phenomenon.

Walter Bennett was an outside right with an explosive shot. Known to one and all as 'Cocky', Bennett was a thick-set right winger, capable of deadly shooting and accurate centres. He joined United in 1895 from Mexborough, after they had secured the Midland League championship. His success with the South Yorkshire club failed to impress a Sheffield journalist who wrote 'From what I know of Bennett, £10 seems a long price to pay'. Undeniably moody, Bennett was a major force in United's great years. He moved to Bristol City in 1905 and was killed in a mining accident at Denaby Main colliery in 1908.

Bert Lipsham joined United in 1900 from Crewe Alexandra. A fast and powerful outside left, his long raking stride and ability to centre accurately at speed created many opportunities for United's other forwards. Lipsham had been educated at the King's School at Chester and became a member of the PFA's first management committee. He went on to play a part in the development of the game in Canada.

A. W. GAMAGE, LIMITED

Largest Cycling and Athletic Outfitters in the World.

REQUISITES FOR Football and all Winter Sports.

THE "REFEREE." 10/6

Also RUGBY. Also RUGBY.

GAMAGE'S REFEREE MATCH BALL

Perfect in Shape. Welted Seams. Waterproof. Every section stretched and hammered. Price 10/6 post free.

Strong serviceable ball, stout cow-hide hand-sewn cases, complete with best rubber bladder.

SPECIAL FOOTBALL BOOTS.

The "GAMKICK," easy, pliable, ensures a firm grip and great power when kicking. Brown Russet Calf. Men's, 8/11. Youths', 7/11. Best Quality to Order, 12/6.

Scotch Chrome, guaranteed waterproof. Men's, 8/6, 10/6, 12/6.

The "UNIVERSAL," Men's 5/11, Boys' 4/11.

The "FORWARDS," Extra Light Chrome, 8/11.

Postage, below 10/-, 6d. extra.

Football Knickers (Wide Legs.)

SHIN GUARDS. (All guards strapped across.)

General Illustrated Sports Catalogue, post free. Orders over 10s. Carriage Paid (unless otherwise stated).

Holborn, London, E.C.

JOHN PIGGOTT,

117 and 118, Cheapside, and Milk Street, E.C.

FOOTBALLS. When ordering say Rugby or Association. No. 3, 4/6; 4, 5/3; 5, Match Size, 6/3 & 7/6; 6, 7/9. Postage, 4½d.

THE SHUREKIK. Studs as authorised by the Association. Price 8/6. Postage 6d.

PLEASE SEND FOR MY FOOTBALL AND GENERAL LISTS.

Drilling &c., in PRIVATE or CLASSES, For GENTLEMEN, LADIES, and CHILDREN. Medical Gymnastics a Speciality at STEMPEL'S GYMNASIUM 75, Albany Street, Regent's Park, London, N.W. (Established 1883). 2 min. walk Portland-rd. Stn. Met. Ry. Finest Gymnasium in England. Open all the Year round. BEST PROFESSIONAL MASTERS.

CRYSTAL PALACE.

Final Tie for the Football Association Challenge Cup.

TOTTENHAM HOTSPUR v. SHEFFIELD UNITED.

Saturday, April 20th. Kick-off 3.30 p.m.

WHITE SHIRTS. TOTTENHAM HOTSPUR.

RIGHT. LEFT.

Goal. CLAWLEY

Backs. ERENTZ TAIT

Half-Backs. MORRIS HUGHES JONES

Forwards. SMITH CAMERON BROWN COPELAND KIRWAN

Forwards. LIPSHAM PRIEST HEDLEY FIELD BENNETT

Half-Backs. NEEDHAM MORREN JOHNSON

Backs. BOYLE THICKETT

Goal. FOULKES

LEFT. RIGHT.

SHEFFIELD UNITED. RED & WHITE SHIRTS.

Referee—Mr. A. KINGSCOTT (Derby).

Linesmen—Messrs. C. SQUIRES (London) and A. J. HINES (Nottingham).

HAVE YOU TRIED "CHAMQUINI WINE"

Manufactured by the ORIGINAL INVENTOR. IF NOT ASK FOR A . . . "LAWSON" THE SAFEST DRINK OBTAINABLE

Was awarded at International Exhibitions held in 1896, 1897, 1899, and 1900, A GRAND and other DIPLOMAS OF HONOUR with GOLD MEDAL AND CROSS.

The Best Tonic in the World.

AT 3D. PER

Write T. W. LAWSON, MANCHESTER,

For Price List, Analyst's Report, and Certified Testimonials.

The "CORINTHIAN" FOOTBALL BOOTS. Hand-Stitched, Light, Pliable, and Easy, Are far in advance of any Football Boot yet produced. Send for Illustrated Descriptive List to the Sole Manufacturers, MANFIELD & SONS, 67 & 68, CHEAPSIDE, E.C. SAMPLE PAIR 10/6 POST FREE. Branches throughout London and Provinces.

BRYAN'S Association or Rugby. Every Ball

FRANK BRYAN'S

The Finest Ball Made.

Extract from the programme for the 1901 Cup Final. Tottenham Hotspur were then in the Southern League. The attendance of 110,802 at the Crystal Palace broke all records and caused astonishment. The match was drawn 2-2, but Tottenham were the victors in the replay held at Bolton.

United's goalkeeper, Bill Foulke, retrieves the ball from the back of the net in the first game of the 1901 Cup Final. The pitch markings were changed at the end of that season.

Harry Johnson, the cheery, hard-working right half was another United player from Ecclesfield. He became a member of the training staff and two of his sons were to play in later Cup Finals for the team.

Picture postcard featuring Harry Thickett. Cards of this size with pictures were first used in Britain in 1899 and offered a cheap, cheerful and quick method of communication. They were sold in enormous numbers in the early years of this century.

Bernard Wilkinson took over the centre half position in the United team in 1901. He was a thick-set man, with boundless energy and eventually took over the team captaincy from Ernest Needham. Always a part-time player, Wilkinson was also a superb cricketer who had to reject terms from the Yorkshire county side, unlike his brother Willie who played for his native county and also played as an inside forward for United.

One year after their defeat by Tottenham Hotspur in the Cup Final, United returned to the Crystal Palace. A portrait of Bill Foulke features on the cover of the 1902 Cup final programme. Foulke and Needham, the team captain, were the top wage earners at Bramall Lane. Foulke's weight had risen to over twenty-two stone by this time (from twelve stone five pounds in 1894) but he was still a superb goalkeeper.

A United attack on the Southampton goal in the 1902 Cup Final. Once again, the match ended in a tie but the 'Blades' ran out victors by two goals to one in the replay which was also held at the Crystal Palace. An injury to Bennett, United's international outside right, gave Billy Barnes an opportunity in the second game and it was Barnes who scored the winning goal.

The United Cup Final team of 1902. This photograph always appears in books of FA Cup winning teams but it is actually the team that faced Southampton in the first game, which ended with the score 1-1. Bennett was injured in the first game and, for the replay, United switched Alf Common to outside right and brought in Barnes as his partner.

Billy Barnes, scorer of the winning goal in the replayed Cup Final of 1902. It seems that no photograph was taken of the Cup-winning side, no doubt because of the unexpected and sudden move by Barnes (a Londoner), who signed for West Ham United a few days after the Final.

Alf Common, a burly, long-striding inside forward with an excellent goal-scoring record, joined United in 1901 from Sunderland. He played a prominent part in the successful FA Cup campaign of 1902 and was capped for England. He refused to re-sign during the close season of 1904, insisting that he had to return to Sunderland for business reasons and United felt they had little option but allow him to return to his former club. If United were upset then, they were doubly annoyed eight months later when Common became the first player to be transferred for £1,000 when he joined Middlesbrough: the fee at that time being regarded as beyond reason.

The new John Street stand of 1902. Dominated by the large, mock-Tudor press box, the new stand provided 3,000 seats and the terrace in front (which was concreted in 1913), holding a further 6,000 spectators. It was designed and built by the Glasgow firm of Leitch & Davis. Archibald Leitch is the only significant name in the early years of football architecture and the John Street stand was his first venture in England and only the second stand he had built.

England v Scotland, at Bramall Lane, 1903. Harry Johnson, the United right half poised next to the Scottish linesman, and Steve Bloomer, the Derby County inside forward, have their eye on the ball. The cricket scoreboard, adjacent to the Shoreham Street stand, is clearly visible.

Arthur Brown, a Gainsborough Trinity centre forward with a hard, accurate shot, signed for United just a few weeks after his seventeenth birthday and was still only eighteen years of age when he was first capped for England. In 1908, United transferred him to Sunderland, in circumstances remarkably similar to those surrounding the transfer of Alf Common. Brown had threatened to give up the game if he was not allowed to return to Gainsborough but, five weeks later, moved directly to Sunderland.

Sheffield United players, 1903/04 season. Ten of these players played for England and one for Ireland. The first eight matches were won and United led the table for much of December and January, but then fell away to finish seventh. The 'golden years' were over.

All-international line up, 1904. Taken on the bowling green, next to the cricket pavilion, the men are, from left to right, back row: Jack Houseley (assistant trainer), Harry Johnson, Harry Thickett, Bill Foulke, Peter Boyle, John Nicholson (Secretary), Ernest Needham and George Waller (trainer). Second row: Walter Bennett, Alf Common, Arthur Brown, Fred Priest and Bert Lipsham. Front row: Tommy Morren and Bernard Wilkinson.

Three

The Interim Years: 1904-1915

Modest seasons end with the Khaki Cup

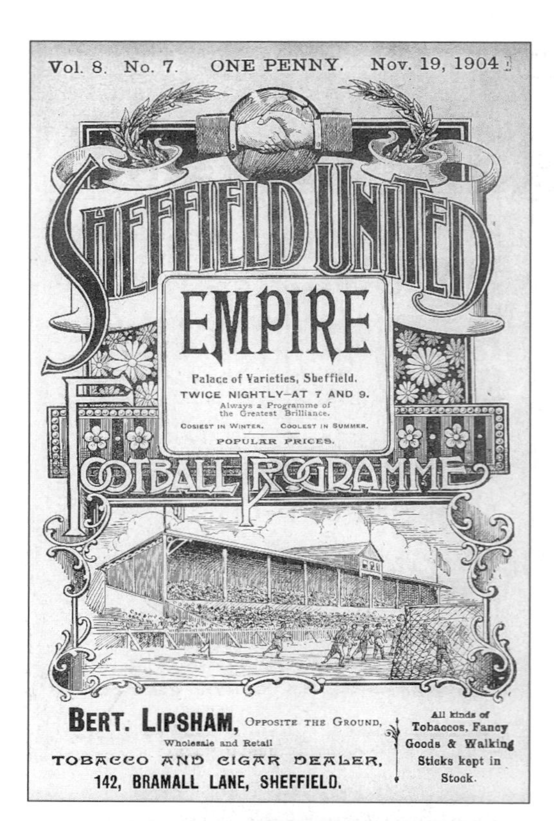

This handsome cover of a 1904 programme included an advertisement for Bert Lipsham's shop on Bramall Lane. The United outside left was transferred to Fulham in 1908.

Sheffield United players, 1905/06 season. The 'golden years' were now over, though no-one connected with the club could have envisaged that for many years to come, a succession of poor cup results and a failure to challenge for the League title lay ahead.

Sheffield United players, 1906/07 season. This group photograph was issued as a supplement to the *Sunday Chronicle*.

A 'picture of manhood' was one contemporary description of Bob Benson, who joined United in 1905 from Southampton. It was thus ironic that Bob Benson should die because of his exertions on the football field: he collapsed during a war-time match in 1916 at Highbury and died in the dressing room. A splendid full back and famous for his penalty kicks where a fellow United player would place the ball on the spot allowing Benson to arrive at top speed before driving the ball into the net. He lost his place in the team because of injury and was transferred to the Arsenal in 1913

Sheffield United players, 1908/09. Among the newcomers was Albert Sturgess, a wing half from Stoke. He was probably already twenty-five years of age when he came to the Lane and held a regular place in the side until 1923.

Joe Lievesley – although he preferred his name to be spelt as it appears on this cigarette card – shown wearing the club's traditional striped shirt, was the first United goalkeeper to wear a jersey different in colour to that of his colleagues, following a change in the laws of the game in 1909.

On a good day, Walter Hardinge was one of the cleverest inside forwards in England, but he was a player of moods and independent spirit. Frequently relegated to the reserve team and then recalled to the first team, he was a 'double' international, playing cricket for England and Kent and winning one cap for football in a match against Scotland in 1910.

Ernest Needham has been added to this line-up of players by the postcard manufacturer. At the end of this 1909/10 season, his playing days came to a close, at the age of thirty-seven, although he continued to serve the club as a scout.

United signed the Welsh international outside left, Bob Evans, from Aston Villa in 1908. It was not until late 1910 that the United Secretary noticed that his place of birth was Chester and, subsequently, Evans went on to win four caps with England.

Joe Kitchen joined United as a young player from Gainsborough Trinity in 1908. Noted for brilliant individual bursts through the opposition, he was equally at home at outside right, as in his normal position of centre forward.

United signed Jack English, a neat and polished left back, from Watford in April, 1913 for £500. English and Bill Cook, his partner at right back, had both played for Hebburn Argyle, a County Durham side.

The first player to join United for £1,000 was Stanley Fazackerley, an inside forward who came to the Lane in March 1913 from Hull City. Tall, slim, stylish and exceptionally clever, he scored regularly with calm authority.

The United players in the summer of 1913. New and better players, including Billy Gillespie, an exciting Irish forward, had joined United but league and cup achievements seemed as far away as ever. A catalyst was required and arrived in November when George Utley, the Barnsley left half, was finally persuaded to sign for and captain United at a record fee of £2,000.

George Utley and Stanley Fazackerley. The team captain played a far more important part in team affairs in the years before the First World War and Utley provided United with a man who could lead by example. A big, bustling player with a strong shot and a long throw, equally at home at wing half or in the forward line, he commanded respect from both friend and foe. Under him, United reached the FA Cup semi-final in 1914 and won the Cup in 1915.

Harold Gough made his debut in the United goal in September 1913 and proved to be as calm and reliable as Lievesley had been, allowing nothing to worry him. He was United's goalkeeper in the 1915 Cup Final and would probably have won a second winner's medal but for his decision in 1924 to become a publican in Castleford, a career move which broke the conditions of his contract

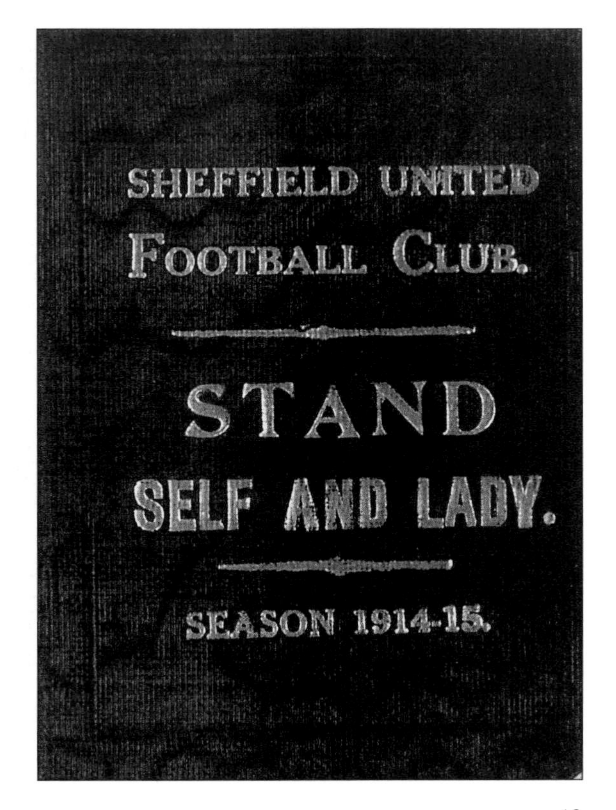

This 1914/15 season ticket, which admitted the owner and a lady to the rear section of the John Street stand. It cost one guinea.

The summer of 1914 and the players are ready for the new season. In spite of the declaration of war with Germany on 4 August, the feeling of the country, encouraged by the government, was one of 'business as usual' and a normal football season ensued. It began disastrously for United when Billy Gillespie broke a leg at Sunderland and missed the rest of the season.

Cup training at Scarborough. Billy Gillespie bravely faces up to Bill Brelsford, the immensely strong United half back. If there was trouble on the field, Brelsford was usually not far away. Showing more discretion than Gillespie are Davies, Cook, Sturgess, Gough, English, Utley and Kitchen.

The team page from the 1915 Cup Final programme. United won the Cup, defeating Chelsea 3-0 at Old Trafford. There had been controversy over the continuation of professional football through the First World War. It had soon became obvious that the war would not 'be all over by Christmas' as had been popularly believed but, in spite of mounting casualties, the authorities decided to complete the Football League and FA Cup competitions.

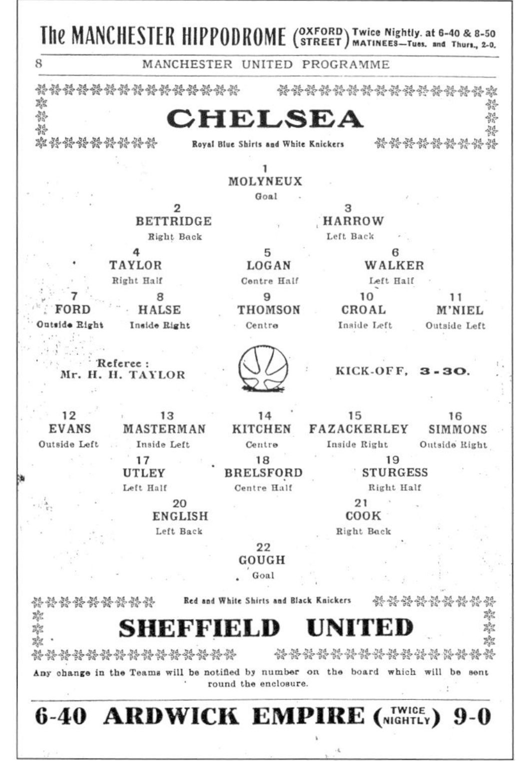

The MANCHESTER HIPPODROME (OXFORD STREET) Twice Nightly. at 6-40 & 8-50 MATINEES—Tues. and Thurs., 2-0.

8 MANCHESTER UNITED PROGRAMME

CHELSEA

Royal Blue Shirts and White Knickers

1
MOLYNEUX
Goal

2 BETTRIDGE Right Back — 3 HARROW Left Back

4 TAYLOR Right Half — 5 LOGAN Centre Half — 6 WALKER Left Half

7 FORD Outside Right — 8 HALSE Inside Right — 9 THOMSON Centre — 10 CROAL Inside Left — 11 M'NIEL Outside Left

Referee: Mr. H. H. TAYLOR — KICK-OFF, 3-30.

12 EVANS Outside Left — 13 MASTERMAN Inside Left — 14 KITCHEN Centre — 15 FAZACKERLEY Inside Right — 16 SIMMONS Outside Right

17 UTLEY Left Half — 18 BRELSFORD Centre Half — 19 STURGESS Right Half

20 ENGLISH Left Back — 21 COOK Right Back

22
GOUGH
Goal

Red and White Shirts and Black Knickers

SHEFFIELD UNITED

Any change in the Teams will be notified by number on the board which will be sent round the enclosure.

6-40 ARDWICK EMPIRE (TWICE NIGHTLY) 9-0

Jimmy Simmons, who scored the first of United's three goals in the Cup Final of 1915. The match was known as the 'khaki final' because of the large number of servicemen in the crowd. United totally dominated the game but it was not until late in the second half, that further goals from Fazackerley and Kitchen secured the victory.

The 1915 Cup-winning team. George Waller (to the left of the back row) had now trained three FA Cup winning teams and would succeed again ten years later.

Four

The Nineteen Twenties: 1919-1929

Cup fighters

The players for the 1919/20 season, the first after the end of the First World War, showed few changes from the Cup-winning side of 1915. English and Evans had retired and Jimmy Revill had been wounded in action in 1917 (he died later in hospital). Only 'Young Harry' Johnson, a dashing centre forward – still in France with Gillespie when the photograph was taken – and left back Ernest Milton, showed any real promise from those players who had their first opportunities during the war years.

Ernest Milton learns the art of the shoulder charge from Bill Brelsford at Highbury. Brelsford had joined United in 1909 and was a totally committed, rugged and reliable wing half.

The 1920/21 season involved United in a long struggle to avoid relegation and the club spent heavily to avoid joining the Wednesday in the Second Division. The first major new signing was that of Fred Tunstall, a speedy outside left with a powerful shot, from Scunthorpe. The £1,000 fee was thought to be a record for a non-League player.

In December 1920, United paid a £4,250 transfer fee, probably a Football League record at the time, to Hull City for David Mercer, an outside right with twinkling feet who had once netted six goals against United in a war-time match. With fine ball control, his model centres would provide plenty of ammunition for other United players in the future.

Sheffield United players, 1921/22. The report presented at the 1921 Annual General Meeting disclosed that £14,145 had been spent on transfer fees and a further net outlay of over £5,000 followed twelve months later. Both were considerable amounts by the standards of the time. Among the newcomers in 1922 were James McCourt, the Third Lanark centre half, and Jimmy Harrop, the very experienced Aston Villa half back.

Harold Pantling had joined United in 1914 from Watford. He was a hard-tackling wing half who rarely had a bad game.

Billy Gillespie took over the team captaincy in 1923. His hairline receded rapidly when he returned to football after serving in the army during the First World War. His balding pate became a frequent feature of the cartoons and caricatures of the time. A brilliant constructive forward, who could also score goals, he had won the first of his record number of Irish caps in 1913.

The FA Cup semi-final, at Old Trafford in 1923 was played before an enormous crowd. The paid attendance was already a record for any match outside of London, before the gates were forced and many thousands more gained admission. With only ten fit men, United were finally defeated by a lucky goal and it was Bolton Wanderers who went forward to the first final to be held at Wembley (and further crowd problems).

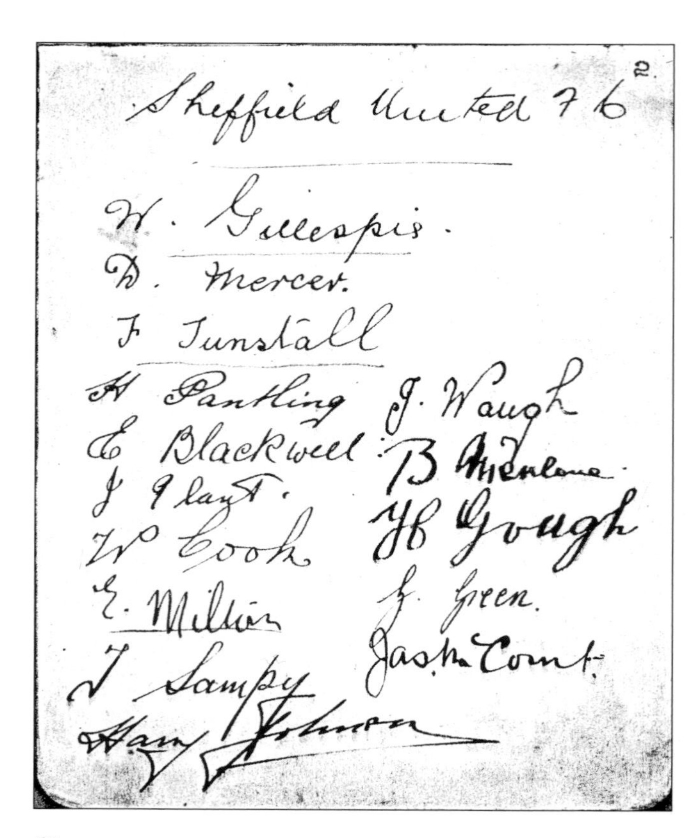

A page from an autograph album of 1924.

Billy Gillespie leads the team out at Leeds Road, September 1924. Ernest Blackwell, the goalkeeper and a local preacher, retired as a player one week later on medical advice.

Just feel that sea air: FA Cup tie training at Scarborough in 1925.

How fortunes can change. United's urgent need of a goalkeeper in 1924 because of Blackwell's retirement and Gough's unwise decision to manage a public house in Castleford, led to the signing of Charles Sutcliffe from Rotherham United. Sutcliffe –seen here with Bill Cook – was thirty-three with a reputation of being no more than a sound third division goalkeeper. Within six months, he was playing at Wembley in a FA Cup final. Wembley gave Cook the opportunity to add a second Cup medal to the one he had won in 1915.

The programme cover for the 1925 FA Cup final.

The Duke of York, later King George VI, greets the United players.

Billy Gillespie with Jimmy Blair, the Cardiff City captain, and the referee, Mr G. Noel Watson of Nottingham, before the kick off.

The only goal of the match came when Tunstall seized on the hesitation of a Cardiff defender.

Fred Tunstall and Billy Gillespie with the Cup. Charles Clegg, the President of Sheffield United and the Football Association is on the right of the photograph.

The 1925 Cup Final team, wearing the shirts chosen specially for the match which bore a badge representing the City of Sheffield coat of arms. George Waller, the trainer, had chalked up his fourth Cup Final success.

The man who missed out. Tommy Sampy signed for United in 1920 and had fourteen seasons with the club. An industrious inside right, who later moved to wing half, his expected place in the 1925 Cup final went to Tommy Boyle. Sampy's brother, Bill, had six years at the Lane but this was mainly in the Central League team.

Outside left, Fred Tunstall, with a selection of his caps and medals.

The old and the new. Billy Gillespie, the United captain, with Jack Pickering and Harry Gooney. United made an attempt, which in many ways was successful, to groom Jack Pickering as Gillespie's successor as a scheming inside forward. He made his reserve team debut on the day of the Cup final. Harry Gooney was the England schoolboy captain that same year and exceptionally gifted. Although he played regularly for United in the early 1930s, he lacked strength and stamina and his playing career never reached the heights that had been expected.

The training staff of Bill Brelsford, George Waller and 'Old Harry' Johnson.

Harry Johnson, United's dashing centre forward who scored a record number of goals for the club, seen at the wheel of his car in Cherry Street with his father in the front passenger seat. Inside forward, Tommy Boyle, and centre half, Seth King, occupy the rear seats. Boyle's father, Peter, and 'Old Harry' Johnson, had both played for United in the Cup finals of 1899, 1901 and 1902.

George Green, totally dependable at left half, won the first of his eight caps in 1925.

Sheffield United players, 1928. From left to right, back row: Sampy, Brelsford, Hoyland, Blair, Alderson, Birks, Waller, Green. Front: Mercer, Boyle, Johnson, Gillespie, Tunstall, King. Matthews is the player featured in the inset image.

Jack Alderson, who had been playing with Pontypridd, succeeded Sutcliffe in the United goal. The United Secretary had been instructed to offer Crystal Palace, who held his Football League registration, £500 if he was not over thirty years of age and the player duly signed, though it turned out later that the new man was nearly thirty-four. He was an acrobatic shot-stopper but was never described as sound or reliable.

Clem Stephenson, the Huddersfield Town captain, waits as Gillespie tosses the coin before the FA Cup semi-final at Old Trafford in 1928. Three dramatic games and five hours of football, watched by record crowds, were required to separate the two teams. The only goal of the third game, a header by Alex Jackson, the Town outside right, came from a disputed free kick.

Vince Matthews, a centre half from Tranmere Rovers, gave his best displays for the club in the Cup run of 1928 and was capped by England at the end of that season.

Five

The Nineteen Thirties: 1930-1939

Depression and recovery

Jimmy Dunne, an Irish centre forward, had joined the Blades in 1926 but it was not until 1929 that he secured a regular place in the team. A fine all-round player, he was the leading goal scorer for five consecutive seasons. A weak defence, however, meant that only a 5-1 victory at Old Trafford in the final game of the 1929/30 season saved United from relegation.

George Waller, the long-serving trainer, finally stood down. Here, his successor, Tom Ratcliffe, supervises this 1930 group of players in pre-season training. A cricket cover can be seen in front of the Shoreham Street 'kop'.

The line-up for 1930/31.

Tom Johnson, his father and elder brother, Harry. Tom began playing as a wing half, but could not hold down a regular place in the team. Later, he settled down as a powerful 'stopper' centre half. Harry moved on to Mansfield Town in the close season of 1931 and continued to bang in the goals.

Outside left Bert Oswald, Bobby Barclay and Bernard Oxley. The economic depression of the early 1930s hit Sheffield badly and football gates fell significantly. United were ill-equipped to buy quality players but they secured a fine inside forward in Bobby Barclay, for £3,500, from Derby County in 1931.

Oxley, Barclay, Dunne, Pickering and Tunstall, March 1932. Tunstall's magnificent career with United ended that season.

United appointed Teddy Davison, the former Wednesday goalkeeper who had gained managerial experience with Mansfield Town and Chesterfield, as their first Secretary-Manager in June 1932. George Green, the player with the ball at his feet, was the team captain and Jack Smith had taken over in goal.

United's failure to win this game at Leeds, in April 1934, meant that their proud record of permanent membership of the First Division since 1893 had come to an end.

United travelled to Dublin, in October 1934, to play Shamrock Rovers. United's first season after relegation was not very sucessful.

'Jock' Dodds, a very raw and robust centre forward, joined United on a free transfer from Huddersfield Town. His dashing style, speed and a mounting goal tally gave United's supporters something to enthuse over. Bobby Barclay looks on, as Dodds wins this game of 'fifty up'.

Sheffield United players, August 1935. This team was essentially that of the previous, disappointing, season. United were in a mid-table position when they met Hull City on the Saturday before Christmas, 1935. A 7-0 victory was start of a twenty-two match undefeated run that took United to Wembley and almost brought promotion.

A record crowd of 68,287 saw as much as the fog would allow, when United defeated Leeds United in the fifth round FA Cup tie. The cartoons by Harry Heap delighted Sheffield football supporters for nearly thirty years.

March 1936 and the United players are relaxing in Torquay.

The team that defeated Fulham 2-1 at Molineux in the Cup semi-final. From left to right, back row: Wilkinson, Jackson, Johnson Hooper, Smith, Cox, McPherson. Front: Davison (Manager), Barton, Barclay, Dodds, Pickering, Bird, Steele (coach). For the Cup Final, Wilkinson, the regular left back, replaced the eighteen year old Cox and Williams was chosen in place of Bird, who had scored the second goal.

The 1936 Cup Final programme.

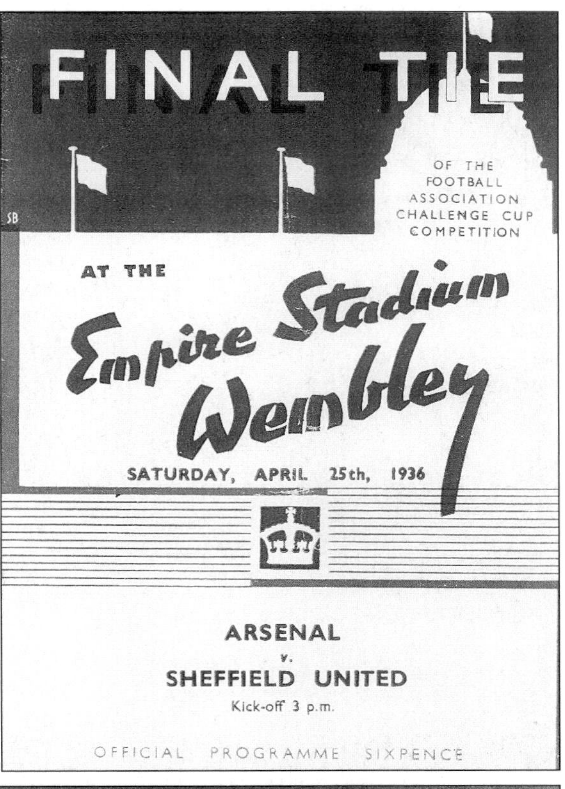

FINAL TIE

OF THE FOOTBALL ASSOCIATION CHALLENGE CUP COMPETITION

AT THE

Empire Stadium Wembley

SATURDAY, APRIL 25th, 1936

ARSENAL

v.

SHEFFIELD UNITED

Kick-off 3 p.m.

OFFICIAL PROGRAMME SIXPENCE

Harry Hooper with Alex James, the Arsenal captain, and referee, Harry Nattrass, before the kick-off of the 1936 Cup Final.

The 1936 Cup Final seen through the eyes of Heap in the *Sheffield Star*.

Jack Pickering made football appear such a simple game. His long passing, which brought both wings into play, was invariably accurate and many of his goals were scored from outside the penalty area with powerful, well-placed shots.

United played a series of matches in Denmark after the Cup Final. This was the club's first tour in Europe: numerous invitations had been received in the past but the board of directors had rejected them because Sunday fixtures were included.

Officielt Program

Sheffield United

mod

Udv. dansk Hold

Onsdag d. 3. Juni 1936 Kl. 19

Idrætsparkens Bane

*

10 Øre 10 Øre

Fodbolde - Fodboldbeklædning

Rigtig Kvalitet. *Rigtig Pris.*

Sportsmagasinet „F. I. B." A/S

Foreningen til Indkøb af Boldspilrekvisiter A/S

Amagertorv 11 - København K

A series of annual cricket matches were held at Bramall Lane in the latter half of the 1930s, between United and Wednesday. The 1937 United team included Cox, Barton, Johnson, Hooper, Pickering and Jack Smith. Among the Wednesday players are Robinson, Millership, Catlin, Hooper and their manager, Billy Walker.

United challenged strongly for promotion in the spring of 1938, only to miss out through their inferior goal average. However, they succeeded twelve months later, although there were several significant changes made to the playing staff during the season. Supporters were shocked by the transfer of Dodds to Blackpool, but the addition of Hampson, Hagan, Henson and Reid to the forward line, eventually swung the balance of promotion in United's favour.

The programme for the final game of the 1938/39 season. United needed a point to secure promotion above the Wednesday, but a goal after ten seconds from Hampson, a hat trick from Hagan and a final score of 6-1 made for a happy afternoon for Unitedites.

Six

The War and its Aftermath: 1939-1952

Davison's new team

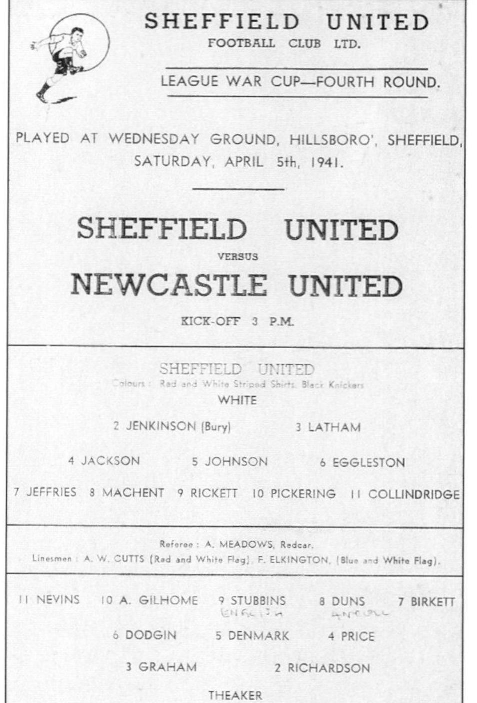

SHEFFIELD UNITED
FOOTBALL CLUB LTD.

LEAGUE WAR CUP—FOURTH ROUND.

PLAYED AT WEDNESDAY GROUND, HILLSBORO', SHEFFIELD, SATURDAY, APRIL 5th, 1941.

SHEFFIELD UNITED
VERSUS
NEWCASTLE UNITED

KICK-OFF 3 P.M.

SHEFFIELD UNITED
Colours: Red and White Striped Shirts, Black Knickers

WHITE

2 JENKINSON (Bury) 3 LATHAM

4 JACKSON 5 JOHNSON 6 EGGLESTON

7 JEFFRIES 8 MACHENT 9 RICKETT 10 PICKERING 11 COLLINDRIDGE

Referee: A. MEADOWS, Redcar.
Linesmen: A. W. CUTTS (Red and White Flag), F. ELKINGTON, (Blue and White Flag).

11 NEVINS 10 A. GILHOME 9 STUBBINS 8 DUNS 7 BIRKETT

6 DODGIN 5 DENMARK 4 PRICE

3 GRAHAM 2 RICHARDSON

THEAKER

NEWCASTLE UNITED
Colours: Black and White Vertical Striped Shirts, Black Knickers

War-time football was run on a regional basis. Clubs drew on players engaged on work in local factories and servicemen on leave and United took the opportunity to give many young players first-team experience. A major disaster, however, struck the club in December, 1940, when the ground was seriously damaged in the Sheffield blitz.

An immediate consequence of the destruction at the Lane was that the home fixtures for the remainder of that season were limited to cup-ties and these were played at Hillsborough.

Two players died during the war: Harold Hampson, who had joined the army in July 1939, and Joe Carr, who was killed at Dunkirk. Young players stepped into the breach: Charlie Thompson had joined United as a seventeen year old in 1937 from Bolsover Colliery. A broken leg in the first leg of a war cup semi-final against Aston Villa in 1944 was a major setback to this strong and fast centre forward.

Many of the old first-team players were in reserved occupations, working in local factories. Right half Ernest Jackson went back to his old job at the Atlas & Norfolk works. Jackson had made his first team debut in 1933 and remained at the Lane until 1949, later joined the training staff. An excellent all-round player, he was very unlucky to miss out on international honours.

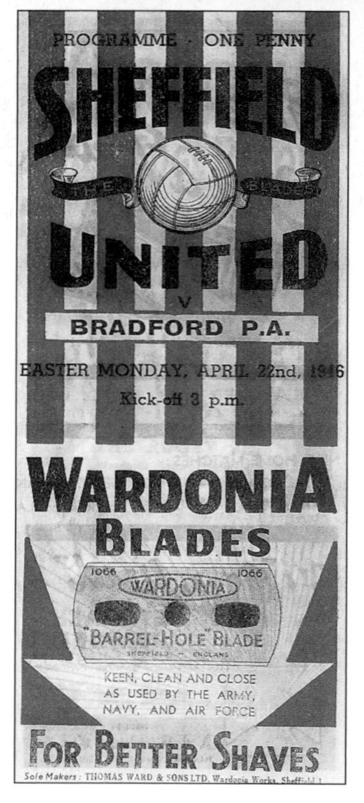

United won the Football League North championship in the last war-time season, 1945/46, with a team that mainly consisted of young players who had come to the fore during the war. The players for a match at Blackpool in February were, from left to right, back row: Stan Machent, Fred Furniss, Jack Smith, Harry Latham, Alex Forbes, Eddie Shimwell. Front row: George Jones, Albert Nightingale, Colin Collindridge, Harold Brook and Walter Rickett. Only Smith and Jones had appeared in the pre-war first team and the whole team had been assembled without recourse to the transfer market.

The last war-time programme to be issued by the club. One sheet of paper, with two folds, provided six rather narrow pages.

United had a satisfactory, though ultimately disappointing season, when First Division football returned to the Lane in 1946. A severe winter and government restrictions on mid-week games took the season on into June. At one stage, the Blades were favourites to win both Cup and League, but fell short of both targets. The players for this match at the Valley were, from left to right, back row: Machent, Furniss, Cox, Smith, Latham, Forbes. Front row: Nightingale, Brook, Collindridge, Hagan, Rickett.

Attendances were large after the war, but United lost a lot of much-needed revenue because they had such limited seating capacity. It was not until late in 1947 that the war-damaged roof on the Kop could be replaced. Harold Brook, seen in this match against Everton, was another of United's war-time discoveries and developed into a fine all-round inside forward.

The star of the side, and undoubtedly the greatest player to wear the United colours in post-war years, was inside forward Jimmy Hagan, who had joined United in 1938 from Derby County. Hagan played regularly for the brilliant war-time England team, but his independent spirit conflicted with the ideas of later selection committees. His place in the England team was championed in the press, both local and national, well into the 1950s, but his genius was ignored. United supporters, at least, will treasure the memories of his brilliant technique and trickery, his vision, industry and memorable goals.

With a powerful shot in both feet and not lacking in pace, winger George Jones might have expected to hold down a regular place in the team, but his playing days were dogged by ill health.

Walter Rickett was another winger who was equally at home on either flank. He had bundles of energy and was totally fearless. Walter was an instinctive player, fine with the ball in front of him, but lost if he had to stop and think. He was transferred to Blackpool in 1948 and later played for the Wednesday.

United trained at Droitwich and used the Worcester City ground before the fourth round FA Cup tie at Molineux on the 25 January 1947. The game finished 0-0 and United won the replay 2-0 at Bramall Lane.

Alex Forbes was one of United's best war-time discoveries. Strong and full of energy, he came to the Lane as a centre forward but developed into a skillful, hard tackling left half. First capped by Scotland in 1946, he was transferred to the Arsenal in 1948.

Colin Collindridge and Stan Machent were two more of the fine players that came to the fore during the war years. Collindridge was a natural left winger: strong and fast with a powerful shot. He was also an excellent header of the ball and was frequently used at centre forward with great success, though it was not the position that he preferred. Machent, a hard working, thoughtful wing half, challenged Jackson and Forbes for a place in the team before moving to Chesterfield in November 1947.

March 1947 brought a sixth round Cup upset when Second Division Newcastle United brought off a 2-0 victory. Tons of straw, which had been laid to protect the pitch from the bitterly cold weather, had to be removed and formed a four-foot high barrier beyond the playing area. The Newcastle captain was Frank Brennan.

The team for the final League match of the 1947/48 season. Jackson, Cox, Young, Hagan and Jones had played in the first team before the war. Fred White had joined United in 1937 as the goalkeeper for the reserve team but did not get an opportunity in the first team until the war and had to wait until October 1947 for his full League debut. 'Paddy' Sloan, the inside right, had joined United as part of the exchange deal that took Forbes to the Arsenal. He only stayed three months before becoming the first Football League player to be transferred to an overseas club.

I. O. M. F. A.

2865

Football Match

SHEFFIELD U.

V

SHEFFIELD W.

Whit-Monday, 17th May, 1948.

KICK-OFF 3-30.

GROUND

TICKET 2/6

THIS PORTION TO BE RETAINED.

ISLE OF MAN FOOTBALL ASSOCIATION. 2865

GRAND FOOTBALL MATCH

(By Special Permission of English Football Association.)

SHEFFIELD UNITED

VERSUS

SHEFFIELD WEDNESDAY

King George V Park, Belle Vue, Douglas, I.o.M.

WHIT-MONDAY. MAY 17TH 1948.

KICK-OFF 3-30 P.M.

ADMIT TO GROUND.

TICKET 2/6

Proceeds for Insular Football.

V.P. Ltd.

THIS PORTION TO BE GIVEN UP.

With the Wednesday in the Second Division, Sheffielders had been denied a post-war opportunity of seeing a derby game. When the clubs did meet, it was in the Isle of Man. The game ended in a 2-2 draw. The Isle of Man FA had instituted an annual match on the island to give Manxmen and women an opportunity to see better quality football.

United returned to the Second Division after their failure to win the final home game of the 1948/49 season. New signings, such as Joe Cockroft, Alec Blakeman, Jack Chisholm and Andy McLaren, were not successful and too much was expected from the new wing halves, Harry Hitchen and Joe Shaw.

Jack Smith had made his first team debut in United's goal in 1931. This County Cup fixture at Oakwell, in May 1949, should have been his final appearance but he returned to play a few more games for the first team in the autumn. He was a splendid goalkeeper and well deserving of his nickname 'Smiler'.

Reg Wright studies the ball control of, from left to right, George Hutchinson, Fred Furniss, Albert Cox, Harry Hitchen and Joe Shaw, while Brook, Jones and Denis Thompson look on. Wright took over as United's senior trainer-coach in November 1949, replacing Dugald Livingstone.

No team could have been nearer to promotion than that of the 1949/50 season, only to lose out by 0.008 of a goal. On the final day of the season, with their fixtures completed, United could only look on as Wednesday played out a scoreless draw at Hillsborough with Tottenham Hotspur and drew level on points with United. A 1-1 result would have left the two city clubs with identical goal averages, but Wednesday were content with the blank score-sheet.

Furniss, Joe Shaw, Latham and Cox stand guard as Ted Burgin punches away a centre at Loftus Road. Burgin's athleticism more than compensated for his lack of inches. Right back Fred Furniss, made his debut at Everton, in 1941, against a background of air raid sirens and gunfire. He remained a calm, reliable member of the defence until his transfer to Chesterfield in 1955.

Teddy Davison resigned from the position of Secretary Manager of United, in June 1952, after twenty years at the Lane. Alf Ringstead and Derek Hawksworth were two of the last players that he signed and they proved to be excellent investments. This team began the season well, with a 5-1 victory at Ewood Park. From left to right, back row: Furniss, Latham, Burgin, Cox, Joe Shaw, Hitchen. Front row: Ringstead, Brook, F. E. Smith, Hagan, Hawksworth.

No United or Wednesday supporters who were there, will ever forget the exciting derby game at Bramall Lane in September 1951. The 7-3 United victory proved to be too much for most of the journalists, who produced some very confused lists of goalscorers. United began the season in storming fashion, scoring forty-nine goals in their first fifteen matches as League leaders, but fell away to finish a very disappointing eleventh.

Wednesday were desperate for revenge and had Derek Dooley in record goalscoring form when the return fixture occurred. Seventeen-year old Graham Shaw made his debut before a record derby attendance of 65,384 and played with a confident manner that would become so typical of his play in the future. Ringstead, the supreme opportunist, put United ahead when this shot from Hutchinson came back off the crossbar, in a 3-1 victory.

Reg Wright leads a training session in front of the old shed at the Bramall Lane end. The players are, from left to right: Burgin, Furniss, Hitchen, Ringstead, Joe Shaw, Hawksworth, Hutchinson, Browning and Cox. Albert Cox had made his debut in 1936 and this was his last season with United. His never-say-die attitude had made him a great favourite with supporters. Jimmy Hagan was now the sole remaining pre-war first-team player.

A group of supporters with rattles, scarves and rosettes are up for the Cup at Southend in 1952. United reached the sixth round but lost a very poor game, against Chelsea, by a single goal.

Seven

Reg Freeman and Joe Mercer: 1952-1958

Up and down and a fresh start

Teddy Davison had suggested to United that Reg Freeman, the Rotherham United manager, should be considered as his successor. The advice was sound and Freeman, seen here (next to the end on the right of the back row) took up the appointment in August with Ernest Jackson as first-team trainer.

Len Browning with Reg Freeman, an experienced manager who built a relationship with his players based on trust.

United moved to the top of the table in November and never relinquished the position. The strength of the team lay particularly in the forward line of Ringstead, Brook, Browning, Hagan and Hawksworth, which scored eighty-three goals.

The top scorer, with twenty-two goals, was Alf Ringstead. The son of a jockey, Ringstead had been born in Dublin and became an Eire international. He was twenty-three years old, playing for Northwich Victoria, when United spotted him and was an instant success when given a first team opportunity. Alf was the ideal winger: two good feet, fast, excellent with his head and a magnificent sense of anticipation which made him all but impossible to mark. For three successive seasons, he was United's leading scorer.

The two inside forwards, Jimmy Hagan and Harold Brook, and Len Browning, the centre forward, each scored seventeen League goals in the championship season and outside left, Derek Hawksworth (seen following Brook onto the field) found the net ten times. Fast, strong and direct, Hawksworth was naturally right footed and played in all the forward line positions with United.

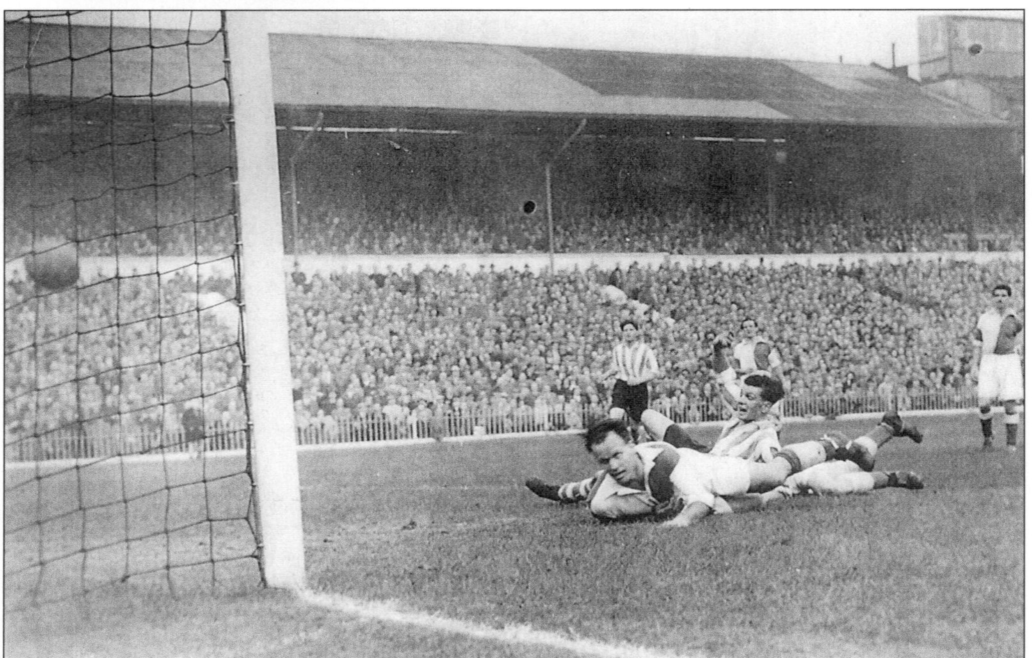

This header from Len Browning gave United the lead in a 3-0 victory over Blackburn Rovers. Albert Nightingale, the former United forward, can be seen to the right.

A. J. Platt, the Club President, congratulates team captain Harold Brook at the championship dinner.

A pre kick-off bouquet for Harold Brook on the 1953 tour of Germany. Burgin, Hawksworth, Browning and Hagan look on.

Work had probably ended rather early for many of the crowd, of over 50,000, who were ready for the 6.30 pm kick off of this Monday evening fixture with Arsenal, in September 1953. Len Browning scored the only goal. Manager Freeman had gone back to his former club and signed a left half, Colin Rawson, but United struggled on their return to the top flight and their cause was not helped by an illness, which ended Browning's football career, and severe financial constraints. The players who defeated the Gunners were, from left to right, back row: Joe Shaw, Fred Furniss, Ted Burgin, Howard Johnson, Colin Rawson and Graham Shaw. Front row: Alf Ringstead, Jimmy Hagan, Len Browning, Harold Brook and Derek Hawksworth.

Team spirit was excellent under Freeman however, and gradually he was able to introduce new blood into the team. Jack Cross replaced Browning at centre forward, Cec Coldwell came in at right back (and began to establish a fine and long lasting partnership with Graham Shaw) while Colin Grainger was beginning to prove quite a handful for defenders as he sped down the left wing. Joe Shaw also began to look a very useful centre half and, later in the season, Tommy Hoyland and Jim Iley were introduced at wing half

The United party in Germany, in May 1955, had good reason to feel optimistic. However, the news of Reg Freeman's death, early in August, was a major blow.

United appointed Joe Mercer, the former Arsenal and England captain, as their new manager but his first season ended in relegation following four successive defeats in April, which included a 3-2 reverse at Villa Park. All three of the Villa goals were scored by Derek Pace, who would later join United and play a major part in a revival of the club's fortunes. Hoyland, Johnson, Iley, Mason and Burgin are helpless as Pace slides home his second goal

Flawed genius. Willie Hamilton was a brilliant young Scottish inside forward who had joined United as a seventeen year old in 1956. His skills were a delight but no club ever solved the problems he had off the field.

Joe Mercer's team building plans began to come to fruition in the 1957/58 season. He built a new defence of: Hodgkinson; Coldwell, Graham Shaw; Richardson, Joe Shaw and Summers – which became a legend in the memories of United supporters of the time

Many youngsters collected the cards issued by sweet manufacturers. Alan Hodgkinson, a brilliant but very reliable goalkeeper, features on this card issued by the A & BC Gum company.

Cec Coldwell, the captain and right back, had joined United in 1951 from Norton Woodseats and worked tremendously hard to make himself a top class player. Very difficult to beat and quick to recover, he was a dedicated and reliable professional.

Graham Shaw had made his first team debut as a seventeen year old before a crowd of over sixty-five thousand at Hillsborough. His stylish play at left back led, inevitably, to international honours. .

Joe Shaw had joined United in 1945 as an inside forward. He made little progress until he moved to wing half but it was as a centre half, with a magnificent sense of anticipation, that he blossomed. Overlooked, for the most part, by the England selectors because he was 'too small', Shaw's play was a joy to behold. He finally retired from the field in 1966, having established a record number of appearances for the club.

Brian Richardson, a very quick and no-nonsense, hard-tackling right half, provided the necessary balance in midfield as a foil to the more stylish Gerry Summers.

The only transfer fee involved for these players was the £3,000 paid to West Bromwich Albion for Gerry Summers. All six members of this United defence were fortunate to suffer few injuries and their contented manager was able to pencil in the same names on the team sheet, week after week.

Billy Hodgson was the first of several newcomers to the forward line. Skilful, terrier-like and a bundle of energy, he became a great favourite with United supporters.

Billy Russell, with Kevin Lewis in support, closes down an Ipswich defender. Russell, an amateur international with pace and goalscoring ability, joined United from Rhyl. Lewis, a fast and hard-shooting right winger, made his debut on Christmas Day, 1957.

On Boxing Day 1957, United paid Aston Villa £12,000 for Derek Pace and the first of his more than 160 League and cup goals for United came after just eight minutes. Pace, seen here between Bill Hodgson and Kevin Lewis, was a most tenacious and honest player with an excellent goalscoring record. Two-footed and an outstanding header of the ball, 'Doc', as he was popularly known – after National Service in the Medical Corps – played with obvious enthusiasm and rapidly became a great favourite with United supporters.

Midway through the 1958/59 season, Joe Mercer was appointed manager of Aston Villa. United finished third in the League (but seven points behind Fulham who were promoted) and reached the sixth round of the FA Cup. Mercer's last significant signing was that of Ronnie Simpson: his speed and powerful left foot added to the team's firepower.

Eight

John Harris: 1959-1973

Gentleman John and two promotions

John Harris, the manager of Chester and former Chelsea centre half, became the new manager at the Lane. 'Gentleman John', as the press often referred to him, took over a fine team.

United led the Second Division table for much of the 1960/61 season. The fruits of the work of the chief scout, Archie Clark (who acted as the senior assistant for John Harris), were becoming evident as youngsters such as Len Badger, Ken Mallender and Tony Wagstaff, who are seated at the front on this pre-season photograph, were added to the playing staff.

The team was strengthened by the addition of the Rotherham United midfielder, Keith Kettleborough, though injuries restricted the number of his appearances.

OFFICIAL PROGRAMME . . . PRICE 6d.

Football Association
CHALLENGE
CUP

SEMI-FINAL

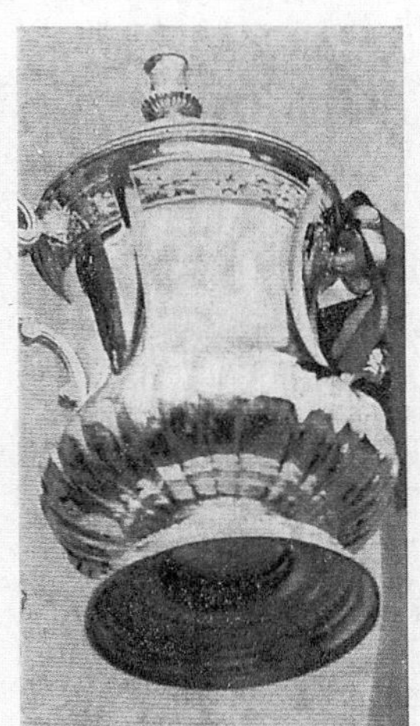

SATURDAY
18th MARCH
1961

Kick-off 3.0 p.m.

LEICESTER CITY
versus
SHEFFIELD UNITED

ELLAND ROAD, LEEDS

United also fought their way through to the semi-final of the FA Cup, but lost out to Leicester City in a second replay.

As March drew to a close, Ipswich Town went to the top of the table as United found it more and more difficult to score goals. Harris made an inspired signing when he paid Swansea Town £12,500 for Len Allchurch, their Welsh international outside right.

Allchurch looks on as 'Doc' Pace volleys a fine goal against Derby County in the match where promotion was guaranteed.

Promotion celebrations, 1961.

Cec Coldwell meets Tony Kay, the Wednesday captain, before the start of a Sheffield derby match at Bramall Lane.

Alan Hodgkinson shows a safe pair of hands to Layne of the Wednesday. Graham Shaw and Cec Coldwell provide cover on the goal line. The cricket pavilion and a packed balcony can be seen in the background.

Derek Pace beats Foster, the Birmingham centre half, to the ball and scores the first of his three goals, October 1963. United led the First Division table for a month, but too many of the team were coming towards the end of their playing days.

Bernard and Joe Shaw keep a close eye on Peter Thompson of Liverpool. John Harris had to build a new team on slender resources. A growing number of young local players, who had first played together in a very successful Northern Intermediate League side, were brought into the first team. Two of the earliest to be given a first team opportunity were Len Badger and Bernard Shaw, who had played together for the 1963 England Youth team.

Len Badger's stylish play and excellent use of the ball brought him many honours, but never a full England cap. He took over the captaincy, from Coldwell, when still only twenty years of age and remained with United until 1976.

Joe Shaw and Brian Richardson's playing careers with United came to a close early in 1966 and a much younger team, of essentially local players, would take the field. Alan Woodward (following Richardson onto the pitch) would be one of the best of those newcomers.

Don Megson, the Wednesday captain, looks on helplessly as Alan Birchenall scores his second goal at Hillsborough in March, 1966. The final score was 2-2. The new Leppings Lane stand in the background was opened in time for the World Cup.

Alan Birchenall scores United's second goal past Harry Gregg in the Manchester United goal, April 1966. Birchenall and his fellow striker, Mick Jones (seen behind the falling Nobby Stiles), were immediate successes when introduced into the first team. The other United player is Barry Wagstaff: he and his elder brother Tony, were two other products of the youth team.

Gil Reece in action at Craven Cottage. John Harris had made little use of the transfer market in the early sixties but the capture of Reece, a fast, hard-as-nails left winger, for £10,000 from Newport County in 1965, turned out to be a shrewd move.

The new Bramall Lane stand, which was opened in 1966, provided some much needed extra seating capacity and was the first major development of the ground since the early years of the century.

The world was shrinking – United visited Latin America in 1966 and 1967. Altitude, heat and humidity made playing conditions very difficult for the United players but local doctors were very impressed with their fitness.

An autumn day at White Hart Lane in 1967. Bernard Shaw and David Munks look on anxiously as Hodgkinson tips the ball over the bar. United supporters had been angry at the introduction of white shorts, in the place of the traditional black, and were even more upset when United became the first club to transfer two players for £100,000: Mick Jones moving to Leeds United and Birchenall to Chelsea.

Colin Addison with John Short, the chief coach, on the old bowling green at the corner of Cherry Street and Shoreham Street. United had signed Willie Carlin, a small but clever and busy inside forward from Carlisle United, then paid Arsenal £40,000 for Addison and, in March, John Harris signed Tony Currie, a talented eighteen year old forward from Watford. United reached the sixth round of the FA Cup but the threat of relegation remained throughout that season of 1967/68 and a poor finish brought Second Division football back to the Lane.

Dick Wragg, the club's chairman, with John Harris and Arthur Rowley. The players were surprised, as they prepared for the new 1968/69 season to learn that Harris had accepted the post of general manager and that team affairs were now in the hands of Arthur Rowley, who had been the manager of Shrewsbury Town. The position of general manager was a new one.

Rowley returned to his former club for his first signing, obtaining the transfer of their captain, Ted Hemsley.

Results on the field under Rowley were disappointing, but his work in the transfer market was outstanding. Eddie Colquhoun was signed from West Bromwich Albion, David Powell, a Welsh international defender, from Wrexham and striker John Tudor from Coventry City.

Colquhoun, a powerful Scottish centre half, was made team captain.

John 'King' Tudor was an immediate success, scoring two goals on his debut at Bury and two more on his first home appearance against Preston North end.

Barry Wagstaff, Willie Carlin and Ken Mallender, seen here at Ashton Gate, were among those that Rowley sold: others included David Munks, Bernard Shaw and Tony Wagstaff.

A day or two after this photograph was taken, in August 1969, Arthur Rowley became the first United manager to be dismissed and John Harris once again took over team affairs. United played splendid attacking football but missed out on promotion.

The story of the 1970/71 season might have had a similar ending to the previous one, but the signing of the Newcastle United reserve goalkeeper, John Hope, and the tenacious Trevor Hockey, from Birmingham, took United back to Division One.

Promotion was not confirmed until the final match of the season with a 3-0 victory against Watford.

Billy Dearden, a forward who had played for Oldham, Crewe and Chester, was twenty-six when he joined United in April 1970. He cost a small fee but his speed, enthusiasm and determination made him a great favourite with United supporters and many famous defenders found him a very difficult man to mark.

A dramatic goal by Tony Currie against Liverpool. United had signed Currie as an eighteen year old in 1968 from Watford and it was immediately obvious that he would be a great player. Extremely clever, difficult to dispossess and with the ability to find his man with long or short passes, he was, without doubt, the finest player to play for United in the last thirty years.

United players meet President Kaunda in Zambia in 1972. A 'good will' tour (but not always on the field of play where the tackling became more than keen on several occasions).

'Woody' in action with Geoff Salmons and Keith Eddy. Alan Woodward made his first team debut in 1964 and will always be remembered as one of the finest right wingers that United ever had. Fast, two-footed and strong, with the ability to shoot and centre with rare power and accuracy.

August, 1973. The scene shortly before 'close of play' of the last cricket match at Bramall Lane. The decision to build a new South Stand and to end cricket at Bramall Lane was to have grave financial implications for the club for the next twenty years.

Nine

Decline and Rebirth: 1974-1989

From Furphy to Bassett

Ken Furphy took up the manager's post in December 1973, with little money available to strengthen the team. These 1974/75 players were surprised, but delighted, to finish sixth in the League.

Keith Eddy was one of several players who came to the Lane from Watford. He proved to be a fine captain and tactician and was sadly missed when he joined the New York Cosmos in 1976.

United still had some fine players, capable of bringing the crowd to its feet. BBC television cameras were on hand to record a 'quality goal' by Tony Currie against West Ham United (the new South Stand is in the background).

After a disastrous start to the 1975/76 season, Furphy was sacked in October. The club's position was hopeless and the tragic season ended in relegation.

Furphy's immediate successor was Jimmy Sirrel. Sirrel was replaced by Harry Haslam, a noted 'wheeler and dealer' in the transfer market, who was appointed in January, 1978. Financial necessity was the order of the day. Tony Currie joined Leeds United and several other players moved to North America. One unusual newcomer was Alex Sabella, an Argentinian forward with brilliant skills. Sadly, this flair rarely produced a goal.

Even in the darkest days, the gritty, determined performances of Tony Kenworthy, provided a ray of light. His first-team debut came in 1976 and his fine tackling and excellent work in the air gave the defence some much needed backbone.

The final indignity for the club and supporters came in 1980, with relegation to the Fourth Division. Happily, the injection of new money into the club and the appointment of Ian Porterfield as manager, brought about a revival. The 1983/84 season ended in promotion to the Second division.

There were new heroes for United supporters to cheer. Keith Edwards, seen here with Joe Bolton and Colin Morris, had the ability to time his runs, lose his marker and finish with a calm authority that made goalscoring look such a simple matter.

Paul Stancliffe came to the Lane from Rotherham United in 1983 and brought wholehearted commitment to the centre of the defence. Appointed captain, he led by example and it was fitting that Premier League status was achieved before his days with the Blades came to an end.

Dave Bassett's first full season as manager brought promotion in the club's centenary season and promise that better days lay ahead.